Farming Once Upon A Time

More Remarkable Photos by J. C. Allen & Son

Dedicated to Chester and Edith Allen

Farming Once Upon A Time

Writers / Editors
Thomas Budd and Claude L. Brock

Photographic Editors
Thomas Budd and Claude L. Brock
in cooperation with Chester P. Allen and John O. Allen

Art Direction
George V. L. Ellis, Donald J. Durs,
Beth A. Doerflein and Pam Jones

Printed in the United States of America

First Printing 1996
Second Printing 1997
Library of Congress Catalog Card Number: 96-84463
ISBN 0-9643429-2-8

Copyright 1996
Concord Publishers
P.O. Box 991099
Louisville, Kentucky 40269-1099
Phone 502-493-0178
Photographs Copyright 1996
J. C. Allen & Son
West Lafayette, Indiana

The Machines

The Crops

The People

The Livestock

Farming Once Upon A Time

More Remarkable Photos by J. C. Allen & Son

1912 - 1952

Concord Publishers

Claude L. Brock and Thomas Budd

A typical day on the square. *1931*

Contents

J. C. Allen & Son
Rural Life Photo Service
West Lafayette, Indiana

J. C. Allen, Founder

J. C. Allen, one of America's most talented photographers, poses in 1919 with the 5" x 7" Press Graflex Camera with which he started a wonderful collection of farm photos.

Introduction

Chester P. Allen (right) and John O. Allen

This book is a pictorial review of agriculture, featuring the photos of J. C. Allen & Son, from 1912 to 1952.

To most people, the excellent photos of the Allens bring back memories of days on the farm as they used to be. Despite the sweat and toil associated with farming in the early years of this century, most memories are pleasant ones.

The late Chester Allen, patriarch of America's oldest professional agriculture photographic firm, and his son, John, agreed to let us publish many of their best photos. They helped us in the selection for *Farming Once Upon A Time*, a process that took some time prior to Chester's death in June 1996. The Allens' archive contains more than 77,000 negatives – by far the most extensive collection covering agriculture in the United States.

J. C. Allen started the business in 1912 at West Lafayette, Indiana, which remains their headquarters. Son Chester spent his career as a photographer, and his son, John, joined the company in 1970. There is no part of the Midwest the three generations of Allens have not traveled. Chester, often accompanied by his wife, Edith, traded-in his automobile every two years when it averaged 75,000 miles.

The Allen photographs really tell the history of 20th Century agriculture in the Midwest. Thousands of their photos found their way into magazines, books, brochures, on calendars, and in many other printed pages for more than 80 years. We found classic photos that have never been used. We endeavored to choose photos that represented changes and progress on the farm from 1912 to 1952, as well as the seasons of the year as they related to farm work.

We have included a chapter for livestock, which was an integral business on nearly every farm. And by all means, we wanted to show the human side, the spirit of the people who made their living from the land which the Allens captured so eloquently.

This book is for reminiscing if you are old enough to recall some of the scenes. It is also for gaining an appreciation of our great farming heritage if you are too young to remember those days when farming was both a way of life and a living.

Thomas Budd & Claude L. Brock

Boys help with arrival of baby chicks. *1932*

Through The Barn Door

The pasture branch is fretting sod-grass seams
The lazy cows lie under dew-drenched willows
Dream of calving time and better meadows.

Jesse Stuart
from Man with a Bull-tongue Plow

Farms were not just farms in earlier days. They were stock farms, and it was the various livestock that made the farm self-sufficient. All livestock required some housing, so the barn was the virtual center of the farming operation.

On many farms, there was more than one barn. It had many purposes. A typical stock barn contained stalls, stanchions, feeders, a feed grinder, granary, hay mow, and maybe even a place for some equipment. If you had a dairy herd, they were usually housed in a separate barn with a milk house.

Beef cattle and hogs were sometimes kept together. Few farms raised enough hogs to afford a separate farrowing house. Sows farrowed in a section of the barn or in individual houses. Chickens, of course, were confined to their own building, referred to as the hen house.

There may have been a horse barn when horses supplied all the power. They had to be fed, watered, and harnessed each day if there was work to be done.

Livestock paid the bills throughout the first half of the 20th Century. They also supplied the table with meat. Every farm was self-sustaining, or nearly so. No one bought milk or eggs. Even corn and wheat were saved to grind meal and flour. A time was set aside for butchering and home curing of pork, an annual event.

Many farmers raised purebreds, and everyone had their favorite breeds. Was it the Duroc or Poland China, or one of the many other breeds of hogs? For beef cattle, it came down to Hereford, Angus or Shorthorn. Some preferred horned cattle, others polled. Dairy producers had several breeds to choose from, and all had their promoters.

Even producers who didn't keep purebred lines wanted a bull or boar with "papers." Such interest in breeding upgraded the quality of all livestock.

Livestock are now gone on most farms in the Midwest, and the barns along with them. Cattle, hogs, sheep, chickens – and yes – horses, are only a dim memory for even those who grew up with various animals. There is something to be said for raising livestock and the pleasures tending to them brought to young and old alike.

Purebred Angus were raised on many farms. *1952*

Straw still used for cattle feed and shelter. *1939*

Filling portable hog feeders on pasture. *1940*

A typical feedlot in 1940.

Father and son feeding ear corn. *1915*

Hogs often followed cattle in the same lot. *1921*

Pigs line up to eat wet feed. *1930*

Feeding hogs on pasture. *1916*

Market hogs being fed in front of shade. *1935*

Horses and sled move the hog waterer. *1942*

Inspecting the pig crop when pigs were farrowed in individual houses. *1935*

Couple milk by hand. *1927*

Ayrshire cows provide a comely scene. *1940*

Before the days of the milk tank truck. *1931*

Silo filling time on dairy farm. *Circa 1950s*

Herding Jersey cows to the milking barn. *1939*

Feeding chickens with bucket. *1942*

The manure spreader was a necessary tool on most farms. *1940*

An early tractor and
manure spreader.
1914

The hen house was a part of most farmsteads. *1934*

Sheep and cattle provided income on this farm. *1943*

There was an art to sheep shearing. *1951*

Steam power being used to shell corn. *1918*

Shelling corn the way it was done in 1916.

Cletrac tractor powers hammermill to grind grain. *1937*

Another feed grinding scene with a Wallis tractor. *1927*

Putting feed in sacks at the grinder. *1931*

Loading ear corn for the grinder. *1936*

Using the corn sheller. *1938*

Marketing poultry in a 1909 McIntyre truck. *1912*

Taking hogs to market. *1918*

Time to go to the stock yards. *1937*

Cultivating soybeans with Massey-Harris 101 tractor. *1940*

Renewal Began With Spring

Young spring grass just after the winter
  Shoots of the big green whisper of the year
Come up, if only for young feet.
  Come up, young feet ask you

Carl Sandburg
from Spring Grass

Everyone looked forward to the arrival of spring. There was no precise way to tell when spring came, but it was generally close to the calendar date.

For some farmers, it was when the frost was out of the ground, and they could take to the fields. Or it may have been when the cows were turned on the pasture for the first time. For farm women, spring arrived when the daffodils bloomed, or when they could hang their laundry on the line again.

Spring was the renewal of life on the farm – livestock, wildlife, plants. It was the spiritual rebirth of those things held dear. Everyone was uplifted with the greening of God's creation after the harshness of winter.

The new season was not always so kind though. There was mud to contend with, and sometimes spring brought troubles, like flooding or a late frost which took their toll on nature.

The dawn of spring always meant taking to the fields. There was scooping and spreading manure which would add nutrients and humus for the coming crops. Oats had to be sowed first, then came corn.

The turning of sod was the most common sign of spring. After the shares were sharpened, farmers hitched the plow to horses or a tractor. Straight furrows with evenly turned soil were the goal of every farmer.

Everyone had an orchard, an important source of food. Blossoms from various fruit trees were the most colorful sign of spring. The garden had to be planted. Baby chicks arrived. Ewes were lambing. Strawberries were the first harvest from the soil, and who can forget that first fresh strawberry pie or short cake.

Spring was a busy time indeed.

Spreading lime. *1923*

Plowing with eight-horse hitch. *1918*

A special rig to drive horses at plowing. *1927*

Plowing with ten-mule hitch. *1931*

Two seedbed trips before planting. *1925*

Sowing seed in the spring. *1930*

Nine horses pull three-bottom plow. *1930*

Liming was a good practice in 1918.

Running the spike tooth harrow. *1934*

Preparing for planting with the harrow. *1925*

Horses still provided power for planting. *1940*

Using a weed rodder. *1922*

Planting soybeans. *1923*

Tractor and mules used to prepare
the soil, while planting corn at the same time. *1919*

Plowing with Oliver plow and 8-16 International tractor. *1923*

Plowing with Silver King tractor. *1934*

Allis-Chalmers WC tractor
and two-bottom plow.
1934

John Deere A tractor and plow. *1935*

Cletrac tractor and three-bottom plow. *1937*

Caterpillar RD4 tractor with plow and drag. *1937*

Farmall F-12 tractor and two-bottom plow. *1936*

Plowing with Farmall F-20 tractor. *1935*

Dealer and farmer with Farmall. *1938*

Plowing with a Case tractor. *1937*

John Deere B tractor. *1947*

Massey-Harris Challenger at work. *1938*

Minneapolis-Moline Z
tractor with plow.
1944

Huber tractor and plow. *1938*

Minneapolis-Moline U and Z tractors at work. *1949*

Ford tractor and mounted plow. *1941*

Allis-Chalmers M
tractor with disk
and harrow.
1933

Oliver tractor pulling subsoiler. *1952*

Rotary hoeing with Case CC tractor. *1932*

Avery tractor and disk. *1918*

Farmall 30 tractor with disk and harrow. *1933*

Case L tractor pulling disk and Case drill. *1934*

Disking with Case RC tractor. *1936*

Single-row disk and new John Deere B tractor. *1936*

Preparing seedbed with Caterpillar tractor. *1939*

Case tractor and corn planter. *1940*

Seeding oats with double drills and Allis-Chalmers tractor. *1932*

Planting corn with Allis-Chalmers U tractor. *1934*

Planting potatoes with John Deere H tractor. *1941*

Planting tomatoes with Ford tractor. *1946*

Drilling soybeans with
Massey-Harris tractor.
Circa 1940s

Cultivating corn with Allis-Chalmers tractor. *1932*

Cultivator mounted on Minneapolis-Moline J tractor. *1936*

Oliver 70 tractor with rubber front tires and steel rear wheels. *1938*

Cultivating and hoeing in one trip with Oliver 70 tractor. *1938*

An early two-row cultivator. *1920*

Threshing next to the barn. *1919*

Summer Meant Haying And Threshing

The wheat harvest was over, and here and there along the horizon I could see the black puffs of smoke from the steam thrashing machines. The old pasture land was now being broke into wheat fields and corn fields, the red grass was disappearing, and the whole face of the country was changing.

Willa Cather
from My Antonia

The lazy days of summer really didn't apply to earlier times. There were always tasks and chores to do, from cultivating the corn to making hay and threshing grain.

It was working by the sweat of your brow, and the days seemed longer than they actually were. Haying and threshing were not easy. Still, they were made more tolerable by a tradition that is all but gone today — neighbors helping each other which eased the burdens.

Sickle mowers came along early and were usually horse drawn at first. They eliminated a great deal of labor. Making loose hay, even with a dump rake or loader behind the wagon, required a lot of hard work. Each wagon load had to be evenly distributed or it could fall. When unloading with fork, rope, and pulley in the mow, everyone had a duty to help speed-up the job.

The first balers didn't make haymaking all that much easier, but they went faster, particularly when used with a tractor. No matter what, you could always count on hot days when making hay.

Most farmers raised some small grain, usually wheat or oats, even if it wasn't the major crop. The binder and steam-powered thresher were a part of grain harvest for a long, long time.

The horse-drawn binder was a common sight, followed by men who put the bundles into shocks. Next came the threshing crew and several neighbors to thresh the grain, usually a dozen or more men. Everyone had a specific job, just as in haymaking. If the weather cooperated, threshing could be completed in a day or so before the crew moved on to the next farm.

Threshing was truly a neighborhood undertaking. The women worked together to prepare the meals. These were sometimes served in the home and sometimes taken to the fields.

The combine eventually retired the steam thresher, and another farming institution became history. Now there is very little small grain to combine in many areas of the Midwest, another change of time.

Deering grain binder at work. *1914*

Samson tractor pulling binder. *1921*

A typical threshing scene with Allis-Chalmers 20-35 tractor and shade close by. *1929*

Titan 10-20 tractor powers separator. *1921*

Unloading stacks of wheat with Case L tractor. *1933*

Loading wheat stacks for threshing. *1931*

Cutting oats with Allis-Chalmers U tractor. *1932*

A day at threshing with
Allis-Chalmers separator.
1934

Cutting wheat with new
John Deere D tractor and
John Deere binder.
1935

Threshing with
Case 22-36 separator.
1935

New 28-46 Rumely separator and Rumely 6A tractor handle the threshing chore. *1934*

Huber HK 32-45 tractor powers a Huber separator. *1935*

Case tractor and Case combine. *1927*

Can you count 10 people
in this threshing scene?
1939

Oat harvest with McCormick-Deering
tractor and Rumely combine.
1929

John Deere tractor and
John Deere combine.
1935

Allis-Chalmers WC tractor and Allis-Chalmers combine. *1935*

Minneapolis-Moline KT tractor and Minneapolis-Moline combine. *1935*

Baling hay out of the barn with stationary baler. *1922*

Loading alfalfa hay by hand. *1935*

The way hay was stored in *1919*

Making hay with bull rake and stacker. *1929*

Hay making in 1919.

Hay loader saves some work. *1920*

Oliver 77 tractor pulls New Idea rake. *1948*

Bull rake and stacker. *1945*

Minneapolis-Moline Z tractor with hay wagon and Minneapolis-Moline loader. *1941*

Hulling clover seed in the field. *1934*

Converting loose hay to bales. *1935*

Best ears go in side box for seed. *1917*

Autumn — Filling The Silo And Crib

Then they began husking their annual crop.
   It had been one of the country's best years for corn.
The long, even, golden ears they were
      stripping the husks from
   and stacking in heaps over the field might profitably
      have been used for seed by any farmer.

Gene Stratton-Porter
from A Daughter of the Land

Autumn and harvest have always been one and same on the farm. However, there are big differences between today and days of yore when it comes to corn harvest.

Harvest was slower and longer in earlier times. It often continued up to Thanksgiving, even beyond. If you had beef or dairy cattle, there was always the silo to fill. It was no easy task. Some silos were taller than others, but they were made of tile, concrete, or wood.

There was an ideal time to make corn silage or ensilage as it was called then. It was when the kernels were dented, while the leaves still showed some green. At this stage, ensilage had a distinct and pleasant aroma all of its own. Several men were needed to make ensilage. One important job was going into the silo between loads and tamping it down. Packed silage cured well and reduced spoilage.

Corn harvest usually took several weeks, depending on the method and the weather. An early frost spelled problems in those days, as corn had to dry standing in the field.

In hand-husking, every farmer had a favorite tool to take the ears and shucks off the stalk. One side of the horse-pulled wagon had several bangboards so the ears would bounce off them and go inside. Shucking about 100 bushels was a good day's work.

The corn picker was a big advancement. The picker increased harvest many times over, when compared to hand-husking. It soon made its way onto nearly every farm. Whether using horses or a tractor, wagons were pulled to an elevator which had to be moved as the crib was gradually filled. The scoop shovel was an important tool in moving corn for generations.

J. C. and Chester Allen captured the energy of silo filling and ear corn harvesting in hundreds of photos. Some of their best follow. While it's a method no one would want to go back to, these photos should bring back memories for some readers, and provide a window to yesteryear for younger readers.

Seeding small grain in corn stubble. *1913*

Headed for the bin. *1927*

Case steam engine used to make corn fodder. *1914*

Part of the corn harvest in 1917.

Cutting soybeans. *1915*

Building corn shocks. *1916*

Drilling wheat with an early method. *1928*

Corn binder at full speed. *1918*

Husking with the bangboards. *1918*

Seeding wheat with team of horses. *1928*

Harvesting soybeans for hay, a tough job. *1928*

rilling wheat with McCormick-Deering tractor. *1929*

Cutting corn for the silo. *1931*

An early seed plant. *1927*

Hart Parr tractor and Avery
combine harvest soybeans.
1930

Gathering ear corn. *1934*

Hand husking in 1935.

Caterpillar tractor with New Idea corn picker. *1939*

Allis-Chalmers
tractor and Allis-Chalmers
corn picker.
1941

Picking corn with Caterpillar tractor. *1940*

Minneapolis-Moline R tractor pulling corn load. *1941*

Filling silo with corn silage. *1939*

Farmall tractor and
Case corn picker-sheller.
1949

Noon lunch break in the field. *1949*

Case tractor and Case corn picker. *1942*

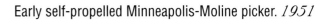
Early self-propelled Minneapolis-Moline picker. *1951*

Allis-Chalmers tractor with New Idea
corn picker and wagon.
1950

Ensiling hay often extended into early fall. *1946*

Friends and neighbors gather for country auction. *1935*

Those Who Found Farm Life The Good Life

Will was very happy in his quiet way.

> He enjoyed the smooth roll of his great muscles,
the sense of power he felt in his hands as he lifted,

> turned, and swung the heavy sheaves two-by-two
upon the table, where the band-cutter madly

> slashed away

Hamlin Garland
from Main-Travelled Roads

The Midwest has been known by many titles — heartland, bread basket, Cornbelt, and prairie — to name a few. All relate to the land in one way or another, and land has long been considered the greatest resource of this mighty region.

During the 20th Century, farmland of the Midwest began to live up to its vast potential as the world's richest producer of food. New farming ideas, inventions, innovations, and practices came to the forefront with man's persistence and perseverance. The farm culture rivaled the industrial culture during the past 80 years of technological advancement.

No historical perspective of 20th Century agriculture could be illustrated without the people who built it. The Allens have captured the vitality of our farms throughout this book, but the most candid portraits of farmers and their families were saved for this chapter.

The period covering the Allens' album has been called "the good ole days." These were tough times with a lot of back-breaking work, for sure, but they also brought farm people together to share and help one another. Farm people took a little time to enjoy the simple pleasures, and to look upon their hard-earned achievements with pride.

No one would trade today's mechanizations for the farm work of the good ole days, but yesterday's values would go a long way toward solving many of today's problems. The Allens caught the spirit and trustworthy ideals of our forthright forefathers and foremothers on the farm. Their subjects were not famous, but they brought agriculture to new levels of achievements.

A pretty girl with her pig. *1928*

Feeding the hens. *1915*

Cool drinking water from the horse tank. *1920*

Going to the field. *1938*

A boy, his trained dog, and the farm horse on a mission. *1931*

A girl and her pony helping out. *1939*

Watering time. *1939*

Placing tile was not easy. *1914*

Proud farmstead. *1920*

Repairing the mower. *1930*

Grandpa gets some help from his twin granddaughters. *1930*

Big peach crop. *1920*

Loads of pumpkins. *1929*

Making apple cider with gasoline engine. *1923*

Finishing a new barn. *1931*

Team of horses move the brooder house to fresh ground. *1931*

Open air school bus. *1927*

Members gather
to cut firewood
for the church.
1934

Delivering grain to the elevator
in a Dodge Brothers truck.
1934

Boy with champion steer. *1949*

The jug of water got passed around on hot days. *1936*

Basting the turkey. *1917*

A good garden provided food for the year. *1939*

Mother gets some needed help with canning. *1935*

Time for music practice. *1938*

Canning occurred throughout the summer. *1923*

Washing as it was done in 1927.

Homemaking was not complete without sewing. *1934*

Parade of stallions at the state fair. *1915*

Big hitch plowing demonstration. *1921*

When families ate their meals together. *1936*

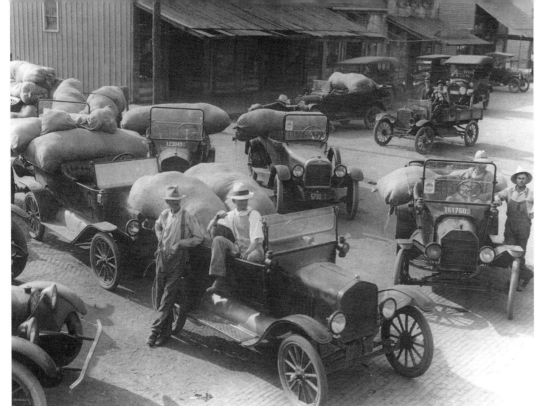

Waiting at the market to sell wool. *1919*

A crop field day. *1921*

An early large team plowing
match drew a crowd.
1929

In a day when the shovel was most useful, unloading lime. *1929*

4-H'ers enjoy recreation at leadership camp. *1936*

Warning to all vehicles. *1917*

WARNING. $10⁰⁰ FINE FOR DRIVING AUTOMOBILES OR MOTOR CYCLES FASTER THAN 8. MILES PER HOUR.

Farm stands were busy places in summer. *1932*

Pride with his tractor. *1936*

Operating the cream separator. *1927*

Pride with his team. *1935*

Method for keeping milk cool. *1932*

All companies were represented at corn picking demonstrations. *1939*